Leader's Guide
to the
Relaxation &
Stress Reduction
Workbook

THIRD EDITION

Martha Davis, Ph.D.

Publisher's Note

This publication is designed to provide accurate and authoritative information in regard to the subject matter covered. It is sold with the understanding that the publisher is not engaged in rendering psychological, financial, legal, or other professional services. If expert assistance or counseling is needed, the services of a competent professional should be sought.

Preface

This guide was specifically designed to assist you in leading groups, using *The Relaxation & Stress Reduction Workbook.* It tells you

- the salient points in teaching stress reduction and relaxation.

- which are the most important exercises to cover, and which are optional.

- a logical order for presenting the exercises.

- the length of time needed for each exercise.

- what materials are needed for each exercise.

- what instructions are needed for each exercise.

- how to integrate *The Relaxation & Stress Reduction Workbook* audiotapes into your program.

- several formats for different lengths of groups.

- the typical problems people encounter when first learning these techniques and suggestions for resolving them.

- how to adjust exercises to fit your group size and environmental specifications.

- how to give clear homework assignments.

- how to review homework in group.

- how to use resistance as a teaching tool.

- how to motivate students to do their homework and continue to use these techniques when the group is over.

This guide assumes that you are already familiar with *The Relaxation & Stress Reduction Workbook,* so it will not repeat the basic concepts and step-by-step instructions found there. For best results, have your students read the workbook as the text used for your class or workshop. The short lectures and exercises you give them in class will then be reinforced by their reading at home.

It is important for you to add material that is of particular interest to you and to your specific group. This will bring special meaning and vitality to the material, and will keep the group and you fresh and involved.

Refer to the bibliography at the end of each chapter in the workbook. Feel free to experiment with and expand upon the material presented here and in the workbook.

Contents

1

Introduction to Relaxation and Stress Reduction

One of the best ways to begin the class is to introduce yourself: talk briefly about how you became interested in the field of stress management and relaxation, what experience you have in teaching this subject, and why you think this is an important topic for the people in your class.

Stress and the Stress Response

Your introduction leads naturally into a brief lecture on stress and the stress response. Be sure to highlight the basic concepts of Chapter 1 in the workbook and include points of relevancy for your particular audience.

Time: 30 minutes

Special Notes

Here are several important points to keep in mind when you give a lecture to the class:

1. The three major purposes of a lecture in this context are to **inform, to clarify misconceptions,** and **to motivate.**

2. Give new information in small chunks so that people can easily assimilate.

3. Keep your message simple. The average audience will not be interested in nor remember more than a few cited research studies. While you will want to provide some historical context and scientific basis for the importance of stress management and relaxation, you will lose a lot of people if you give them an academic treatise.

4. Gear your message to the educational level and interests of your audience.

5. Make your message encouraging. Cite personal or clinical anecdotes and studies which indicate that your concepts are grounded in experience and that your techniques work.

6. Provide an opportunity for class members to ask questions. It's best if you let people know before you start lecturing whether you want to answer their questions as you go along or at the end of your talk.

7. Make it clear before you start answering questions that the purpose of a stress management and relaxation class is to teach general concepts and techniques which have universal relevancy, and not to address the details of an individual's particular life situation. It is hoped that in the process of learning these general skills the individual will solve many of his own specific problems or clarify the need for one-on-one professional help.

8. Since the individual student will relate to the general concepts and techniques in terms of his specific situation, he will often bring up questions and comments particular to his life experience. This can benefit him and the class as long as it throws further light on the basic stress management concepts and exercises. It is important for the leader to interrupt people who want to talk at length about their symptoms and problems. You can relate these individual examples to general stress management concepts, and then redirect the class to stress management skill building. Examples of how to do this are as follows:

    "That brings up an important point, Mrs. Cook." Then follow up this statement with how her problem or symptom is a good example of stress or a stress response.

    *

    "You sound pretty discouraged, frustrated and angry about the unfair treatment you are getting at work. What stress management tools have you learned thus far that you think might help you deal more effectively with your reaction to this stress?"

    *

    "You must be my straight man today, John, I was just about to bring up the topic of 'Job Stress.'"

    *

    "Betty, I know that your husband and children really get on your nerves, and you have discovered that the stress reduction technique of just talking about it reduces your frustration level and tension headaches. Rather than use the group to ventilate your feelings, I'd like to see you begin to make some new friends with whom you can share your feelings and get emotional support. Social networks serve as a buffer against the stresses of life."

9. At some point during the first session, you may want to give the class logistical information. This information can be in written form and referred to in as little or much detail as you prefer. Typical logistical information includes:

    *   the name of your class or workshop
    *   your name

- when the class session is to begin and end
- the total number of sessions
- the date of the last session
- holidays when the class will not meet
- when you plan to take a break during the session
- location of rest rooms and smoking areas
- your expectations regarding confidentiality
- your expectations regarding audiotaping
- your expectations regarding attendance and punctuality
- your expectations regarding class participation
- your expectations regarding homework assignments
- instructions regarding how to get credit for the class
- requirements for those taking class for credit
- name of text and where it can be purchased
- list of topics to be covered
- the learning modalities to be used:
    lecture
    demonstration of exercises
    practice exercises in class
    discussion and questions
    practice exercises at home
    monitoring own experience and progress
    reading text at home
    audio cassette tapes

10. At this point, the group members are clear about what they are going to learn, why you think that it is important, and how you intend to conduct the class.

Exercise: Schedule of Recent Experience

Purpose:
1. Allows individuals to get acquainted.

2. Enables individuals to acknowledge to themselves and others the major stresses in their lives.

3. Underscores the relationship between cumulative stress and the possibility of major illness.

Time: 30 minutes

Materials:
If students do not have their own copies of *The Relaxation & Stress Reduction Workbook* yet, give each group member a copy of the Schedule of Recent Experience sheets on pages 5 to 8. Provide extra pencils or pens for those who do not have one.

Instructions:
1. You can use the introduction to the Schedule of Recent Experience on page 4 in the workbook. Remind the class that one definition of stress is "any change to which you have to adjust."

2. Go over the instructions on pages 5 through 8 in the workbook, and then answer questions.

3. Tell students to raise their hand if they have a question as they go along, and you will come over and assist them.

4. Instruct students who finish early to get up and take a break without disturbing those who are still working.

5. When everybody is finished scoring the inventory, call the class back to order.

6. Have students break into small groups of three or four people, introduce themselves, and share what they learned about themselves in taking the Schedule of Recent Experience. Have one person in each group volunteer to later report back to the large group anything particularly interesting or any unanswered questions that came up in his group.

7. Two minutes before the end of the allotted time, give people a two-minute warning to wrap it up.

8. Have the small groups reassemble into one large group. Then ask each one of the small group reporters to share what his group learned that was particularly interesting and any questions that remained unanswered. During this discussion, be sure that the following points are covered:

- Changes can be big or small, positive and/or negative.
- Having to adapt to change is stressful.
- The stress of change is cumulative.
- The amount of change a person experiences may be predictive of future illness.
- Just because a person received a high score doesn't mean that he has to get sick; he can do many things to help prevent illness and stay healthy.

Other points to include

- The range of scores given for the Schedule of Recent Experience is based on a hospital population. Persons who received high scores were people who tended to get sick more frequently than people with low scores. This is only a correlation. Critics of the Schedule of Recent Experience would argue that it does not necessarily show cause. There are many other factors that contribute to whether a person is likely to become ill, such as genetic predisposition; stabilizing influences (i.e., a good social network, a pleasant home life, a satisfying job, a regular exercise program); and how people perceive the stresses in their lives and their ability to respond to those stresses.

- Typically, there will be a few participants who will score low on the Schedule of Recent Events but who are ill or worn out. Have these people fill out the inventory again, this time for the year preceding the past year. It is likely that their second score will be higher than their first. A frequent comment from these people is that they really needed this class one or two years ago, but were too busy just trying to survive.

- Given that we cannot go back and re-choose our parents, stress management focuses on what we do have some control over: our thoughts, feelings and behavior, and to a lesser extent our environment.

Symptom Checklist

Purpose:
1. This inventory will help individuals identify their stress symptoms and decide how uncomfortable each of these symptoms are.

2. At the end of class, students can fill out the checklist a second time to determine how much symptom relief they were able to achieve with the tools they learned in this class.

Time: 10 to 20 minutes

Instructions:
1. See pages 10 and 11 in the workbook.

2. This inventory can be filled out in class or given as homework.

3. After your students have completed this inventory, call for questions and comments.

4. Optional: Read off the symptoms and have people raise their hand if they gave themselves a three or higher on a particular item. This is useful information for you. It will also give your students a sense that they are not alone in their particular brand of suffering.

5. Optional: Let people form dyads to briefly discuss their symptoms of stress. Limit this to about four minutes.

Symptom Effectiveness Chart

Purpose:
1. This chart gives a rough overview of the most effective stress management and relaxation techniques for relieving specific symptoms.

2. This is an excellent way to give a quick overview of what you plan to cover in your course.

3. It is interesting to review this chart with the class at the last session, asking individuals which tools they thought were most useful in relieving their stress symptoms. This can be done efficiently with a show of hands. This discussion provides useful information for you as you consider how you will improve your classes in the future.

Time: 5 minutes

Instructions:
1. See pages 12 and 13 in the workbook.

2. Show your students how to read the chart.

Note:
While the techniques that are most effective in treating a specific symptom are marked with an "X," students must take into account their individual situation in deciding which tools will help them. For example, Lonnie's major symptom of stress is obesity due to compulsive eating. Obviously, she needs to work on nutrition and exercise. But she also needs to ask WHAT TRIGGERS her compulsive eating. If she eats because she is a perfectionist who often fails to achieve her high expectations, she needs to look at "Refuting Irrational Ideas" (Chapter 10). If she eats because she has difficulty saying "no" to people, asking directly for what she wants, dealing with criticism from others, or expressing her feelings and opinions, then she needs some "Assertiveness Training" (Chapter 12). If she tends to give up her diet or exercise program at the first temptation or hardship, she will benefit from "Coping Skills Training" (Chapter 11). If she eats to relax and dampen her anxiety, then she would benefit from learning relaxation techniques. The Stress Awareness Diary, in "Body Awareness" (Chapter 2), is a useful tool for students who want to learn more about what triggers their symptoms of stress.

2

Body Awareness

Exercise: Body Inventory

Purpose: Promotes awareness of body, especially tension areas.

Time: about 25 minutes

Instructions:

1. See pages 15 to 17 in the workbook.

2. *Optional:* Play the 21-minute New Harbinger Publications audio cassette tape on Body Inventory, which will take the class through the following three exercises: *Awareness, Body Scanning,* and *Letting Go of Your Body.*

3. Give a brief introduction to Body Awareness.

4. Take the group through the Awareness exercise, one step at a time.

5. Go directly on to the exercise on Body Scanning.

6. Make it clear that people do not need to close their eyes to do this exercise; it just makes it easier to focus inward. Some people are fearful of closing their eyes around strangers. A few are even fearful of closing their eyes when alone at home to do something new such as these exercises.

7. Be sure to give people enough time to follow one instruction before moving on to the next one. A good way to judge this is by doing the exercise along with the class.

8. *Optional:* After completing the first two awareness exercises, have members of the group turn to a person sitting next to them and share what they became aware of that they were not aware of before doing the exercises. Give each person a minute or so to respond.

9. The exercise on Letting Go of Your Body does not require participants to lie down. If they are sitting in chairs, specifically instruct them to take everything off their laps, rest their feet flat on the floor, and put their hands in their laps. Invite them to close their eyes, if they wish. Follow the instructions in the workbook, remembering to allow ample time for people to comply.

10. After completing the Letting Go of Your Body exercise, have group members turn to the person sitting next to them and share what they became aware of that they were not aware of before doing this exercise. Give each person a minute or so to respond.

11. Call for questions and comments.

12. These three exercises are presented in this order because they build on one another and ask the participant to do progressively more challenging things. The exercises can, however, be presented separately or in conjunction with other relaxation exercises. If you have time to do only one of these exercises, do Body Scanning.

13. Encourage people to practice these three Body Inventory exercises each day on their own. Good times to practice are when they go to bed, before getting up in the morning, when they are having to wait, during a work break, or any other naturally occurring lull during their day when they are free to turn their attention inwards. The other option is to schedule an appointment with themselves to do a Body Inventory each day at a particular time.

14. Tell members to use the Record of General Tension described on workbook page 19 to keep track of their tension level before and after they do Body Inventory exercises. In this way, they can monitor their progress and remind themselves to do the exercises regularly.

15. *Optional:* Have your students use the Record of General Tension to monitor their progress on all relaxation homework assignments.

Exercise: Stress Awareness Diary

Purpose:
1. The diary is a homework tool that allows students to monitor their awareness of their symptoms and stresses throughout the day.

2. The diary identifies how particular stresses result in predictable symptoms.

Time: 5 minutes to explain in class.

Materials: Several pieces of paper and a pen or pencil.

Instructions:
1. Have the participants follow the instructions in the workbook on pages 17 and 18.

2. Many people find that it is excessive to keep the diary for two weeks. Students who keep a diary for two or three days during a week and one day on the weekend net some very useful data. For this exercise, it is best to set a minimal expectation for homework, and let people exceed it.

3. Tell your students that they will have an opportunity to go over their Body Inventory exercises and Stress Awareness Diary at the beginning of the next session.

4. Start the next session by having participants gather in groups of three or four to discuss how each person fared with the assignments.

   • Instruct the people who did their assignments to describe any connections they observed between specific stresses in their lives and their symptoms of stress. Ask them also to comment on their experience with the Awareness exercises and their Record of General Tension.

   • See Chapter 21 in this guide for suggestions on how to deal with people who do not do their homework.

   • Have one member from each small group report on how many people did the homework, and any interesting observations or unanswered questions when the large group is reconvened.

3

Progressive Relaxation

Exercise: Progressive Relaxation

Purpose:
Deep relaxation without the aid of imagination or will power. All it takes is simple, mechanical tensing and relaxing of major muscle groups.

Time: About 30 minutes

Instructions:
1. The instructions in the workbook on pages 21 to 25 are quite complete.

2. *Optional:* You can use the 22-minute audio cassette on "Progressive Relaxation" by New Harbinger Publications to take the class through Progressive Relaxation. This way you are free to demonstrate the technique as the tape describes what to do. You are also able to walk around the room during the exercise and correct individual problems.

3. *Optional:* You can model your own presentation of Progressive Relaxation from the audio cassette. This will help you establish proper timing.

Special Notes

While progressive relaxation can be practiced in a chair, it is best to practice in a recliner, bed, or on a comfortable rug or blanket on the floor. The reason is that when you instruct a person to let go, they ideally should be able to let go without worrying about hitting a hard surface, hurting themselves, placing their hands on their legs, or making a loud noise. Make clear to your students that they are learning this technique in a less than ideal setting, and that it will be much easier to do at home.

You will need to move around the room and observe each person practicing this exercise in order to make corrections.

The most obvious mistake that people make when they are first learning this technique is to slowly bring their arms or legs down. This is an indication that they are not letting go of the tension in their arms. This is easily corrected by you demonstrating, using exaggeration, "letting go" of your arm tension in a *controlled* slow way and then "letting go" by letting your arm fall *limply* to your side. Immediately let them try to do it correctly.

Encourage people who do not tense enough to tense more, and suggest to those who are obviously overly straining to tense less.

Tell class members to be cautious with any part of their body that has been previously injured or is otherwise weakened. Pain is an indication that they are tensing too hard.

Reassure people that tingling, jerking, needlelike sensations, "surging," and warmth are all normal sensations associated with tensing and relaxing.

After you have taken the group through the basic procedure of Progressive Relaxation, have participants form dyads for three minutes of sharing. Answer questions when the groups combine into one.

Encourage people to practice Progressive Relaxation twice a day for 15 minutes. Almost all participants express some immediate benefit from this exercise, and within a week or two most people report attaining profound relaxation in less than 15 minutes.

Have group members keep track of their level of tension on the 10-point scale described on page 19 in the workbook before and after they do Progressive Relaxation at home.

Once people have mastered the long form of Progressive Relaxation (this usually takes a week or two), have them practice the short form twice a day.

When students have mastered the short form of Progressive Relaxation, suggest that they use it at times during the day when they are tense: when they are waiting, during a mini work break, before they start driving, after a stressful interaction, or before they go to sleep.

This is a powerful relaxation exercise and easy to learn. It should be included in any abbreviated stress management program.

4

Breathing

Perhaps because people take breathing for granted, beginning with a lecture on breathing is a waste of time. Skip right to the exercise on Breathing Awareness.

Exercise: Breathing Awareness and Deep Breathing

Purpose:
1. Enables a person to discover how he currently breathes.
2. Points out the most obvious bad breathing habits.
3. Develops awareness of how the chest, diaphragm, and abdomen each play a role in the breathing process.
4. Facilitates deep, relaxing breathing.

Time: 15 minutes

Instructions:
1. Follow the instructions for the Breathing Awareness exercise on page 29 in the workbook. Ideally, this exercise should be done lying down, in loose clothing, and on a blanket or rug on the floor. If this is not possible, have participants do the exercise in their seats. Start with instruction number two in the workbook.

2. You may need to move around the room to make sure that people have their hands placed correctly.

3. After completing instruction number six of the Breathing Awareness exercise, skip to number four of the Deep Breathing exercise. Assure people that it is all right to breathe through their mouth if they are unable to breathe through their nose.

4. Have your students practice instruction number five of the Deep Breathing exercise for a few minutes. Then instruct them to continue practicing deep breathing while you tell them about the importance breathing plays in their lives. This is a good time to go back to the introduction on breathing that you skipped, and simply and slowly describe the process of breathing. When you are finished, tell the group you would like them to continue deep breathing for a few more minutes and that you will indicate when the class will continue on to another exercise. Do not tell people to stop deep breathing as a way to end this exercise.

5. Draw this exercise to a close by suggesting instructions number seven through nine of the Deep Breathing exercise.

6. *Optional:* People are usually quite relaxed at this point and could use a short break.

7. Call for questions and comments.

8. Suggest that people practice this Breathing Awareness and Deep Breathing exercise once or twice a day for five to ten minutes at a time. Remind them that it is easier to practice lying down, but can easily be done while sitting.

Enlivening Breathing Exercises

Purpose:
These exercises can be done alone or in any combination for the purpose of energizing the group. You may choose to teach these exercises all together, or save them and dole them out when everyone's attention seems to be drifting.

Time:
Each of these exercises takes less than 5 minutes to learn and practice.

Space Requirement:
With the exception of Complete Natural Breathing and the Purifying Breath, people need to stand, unencumbered by chairs, at least an arm's length apart.

Instructions:
1. Begin by teaching Complete Natural Breathing and the Purifying Breath, following the instructions on page 31 of the workbook. Assure people who cannot breathe through their nose that it is all right to breathe through their mouth for these exercises.

2. Then go on and teach one or more of the following exercises: *Tap Away Tension, The Bracer, The Windmill,* and *Bending* described on pages 32 and 33 of the workbook.

3. Suggest that people practice these exercises when they need a lift at home or at work.

Optional Breathing Exercises

• The *Relaxing Sigh* is a great natural way of releasing tension and can be practiced anywhere.

- *Complete Natural Breathing and Imagination* is a sample of how breathing techniques can be combined with mental pictures to enhance energy, reduce pain, and assist in the healing process.

- *Alternative Breathing,* last but not least, is extremely relaxing and particularly effective in relieving tension and sinus headaches. The one problem with this exercise is that it requires relatively clear nasal passages. Have people do this exercise as slowly and gently as they can. It is unlikely class members will do this exercise unless you demonstrate it to them, because the instructions, while simple, appear complex.

Special Notes:

1. Demonstrate each of the breathing exercises as you describe them.

2. Repeat the instructions two or three times while people are practicing these exercises.

3. Walk around the room and identify and correct obvious problems individuals are having.

4. At the completion of each exercise, answer questions about that exercise before going on to the next one.

Audiotape

The New Harbinger Publications 18-minute cassette tape on Breathing is divided into four segments, which you can use to teach the following exercises:

1. Deep Breathing
2. Two short energizing breathing exercises
3. Complete Natural Breathing
4. Alternative Breathing

5

Meditation

As with breathing, it is more important for people to experience meditation than understand it intellectually. However, unlike with breathing, focusing on one thing at a time seems foreign and difficult to Westerners. So a brief introduction to Meditation will help to familiarize your audience with the fundamental elements common to all forms of meditation, the historical background of meditation, and the scientifically proven benefits of it.

Introduction

Purpose:
Meditation can be a profound form of deep relaxation in which the individual attempts to focus his attention on one thing at a time.

Time: 5 minutes

Instructions: See pages 37 and 38 in the workbook.

Environment:
People can practice meditation on the floor, on cushions, or in chairs. Soft lighting and a comfortable room temperature are ideal. A quiet atmosphere is preferred, but not necessary. Suggest that extraneous sounds are part of the natural environment to be noted and then let go of.

The exercises in the workbook are divided into five groups.

Group 1. Three Basic Meditations

Time: 30 minutes

Instructions:
1. At the very least, you will want to teach your students how to establish their posture, to center themselves, and to do the three basic meditations. Instructions are on pages 39 to 45 in the workbook.

2. At the beginning of the meditation exercises, let people know that should they feel particularly uncomfortable with one of the exercises, they can modify the instructions, or simply stop doing it. They can just sit and relax until the exercise is over. If necessary, they can get up, go outside and walk around. Encourage people to try the exercise again on their own, after they have had an opportunity to sort out their discomfort and to ask questions.

3. The Breath Counting Meditation is an ideal exercise to begin with because it builds on the students' recently acquired knowledge about breathing and therefore seems familiar. It is easy and it is deeply relaxing.

4. Then teach Mantra Meditation. Remind the students that they can use any sound that they feel comfortable with for their mantra. Have them chant "OM" aloud as a group for a few minutes. Then have them repeat their mantra to themselves for a few minutes. Ask participants to compare for themselves the difference in their bodies between chanting aloud versus in silence. Ask which is more relaxing?

5. In teaching the Gazing Meditation, you may choose to furnish some items to contemplate, such as a blue glass vase, a candle, an abstract carving, or a natural object. Have the large group break into small circles, so that participants can gaze at one of these items from a comfortable distance. Or you may prefer people to contemplate something that they brought with them, such as a pin, ring, or coin. In this case, nobody has to move.

   Typical problems that people encounter with Gazing Meditation include:

   • **Eye strain.** Reassure students that it is all right to blink. Remind them not to stare at the object, but rather softly explore it with the eyes. Some people prefer to take out their contact lenses when they do this exercise. Do not do this exercise for more than five minutes at first. Suggest increasing the time on this exercise, but only as comfortable.

   • **Visual illusions.** Most people react to these with interest, some with alarm. Explain that illusions are common and that they are to be noted and then let go of rather than become distracted by them.

6. Review Special Considerations on page 44 of the workbook.

7. Form small groups of three or four to let people discuss their experiences with these meditation exercises. Which did they enjoy the most and why? What difficulties did they encounter? How did they deal with them? After five minutes, have the group assemble into one group and let each small group representative give a brief summary of the important points and questions brought up. Address any unresolved questions or problems.

8. Suggest that your students select one of these forms of meditation to practice 10 to 20 minutes, once or twice a day for a week, and then decide if they want to continue this form of meditation or try another.

Group 2. Releasing Muscular Tension

Time: Up to 5 minutes each.

These exercises are essentially Body Awareness exercises. You may choose to include them when you discuss Body Awareness. They are optional meditation exercises. See the instructions in the workbook on pages 45 and 46.

Group 3. Softening

Time: Up to 5 minutes each.

The first of the three exercises in this group is especially useful in suggesting a way to deal with uncomfortable feelings and sensations that are bound to come up during meditation, or for that matter, any time. The other two exercises are variations on the same theme and are optional. See the instructions in the workbook on pages 46 to 49.

Group 4. Being Present in the Present

These are three optional exercises that teach the individual to focus his attention on the here and now. These exercises can be practiced anywhere, but for best results they initially should be practiced with minimal disturbances. The instructions for these exercises are simple to follow. They are in the workbook on pages 49 to 52. You may choose to do the Walking Meditation with the class, if you have the space. Ideally, you can suggest that individuals try these meditations on their own in their daily life and then report back to class in the next session what their experiences were like.

Group 5. Letting Go of Thoughts

Time: 5 minutes

This is a powerful exercise that teaches the individual to observe his or her flow of consciousness without becoming caught up in it. It underscores the unruly nature of our minds: how thoughts and sensations appear seemingly from nowhere and become all-consuming if we let ourselves dwell on them. It is suggested as an optional exercise because most people find it difficult, and a few don't stay with it long enough to experience its benefits. The instructions for this exercise are on pages 52 and 53 of the workbook.

Special Notes:

1. Suggest to your students that they can gradually expand the practice time of each of these exercises as feels comfortable.

2. Same as Instruction 8 under Group 1.

Audiotape

The New Harbinger cassette tape on Meditation is 38 minutes long. It is based on the first edition of *The Relaxation & Stress Reduction Workbook* and does not closely adhere to the Meditation chapter in the third edition. It includes the following ten segments:

1. Introduction to Meditation
2. Posture, Centering, Scanning for Tension, and Letting Go
3. Yoga Awareness Exercise
4. Problem Solving
5. Breath Counting
6. Mantra Meditation
7. Contemplation
8. Yantra Meditation
9. Lotus of a Thousand Petals
10. Visualizing One Thing at a Time

6

Visualization

Introduction

Purpose:
This chapter would have been better named "Imagination," for it describes how to use all of your senses to tap your own creative resources for guidance, healing, stress reduction, and relaxation.

Time: 5 minutes

Instructions:
1. See pages 55 to 58 in the workbook.

2. When introducing this topic, you will probably want to mention some of the fascinating work of Emil Coue, Carl Jung, Stephanie Matthews, O. Carl Simonton and others. Briefly describe the three different kinds of visualization for change, as well as the rules for effective visualization.

Basic Tension and Relaxation Exercises

Present the three basic tension and relaxation exercises—**Eye Relaxation, Metaphorical Images,** and **Creating Your Special Place,** and the two optional exercises—**Finding Your Inner Guide** and **Listening to Music.**

1. Eye Relaxation (Palming)

Time: 5 minutes

Instructions: See page 58 in the workbook.

Note: Many people assume that they are not imaginative and therefore will perform poorly on the visualization exercises. This is a good visualization exercise to begin with, because it does not rely on imagination. Rather, it allows the individual to relax and observe natural phenomena. Hence, it's almost impossible for anyone to "fail" with this exercise.

2. Metaphorical Images

Time: 8 minutes

Instructions: See page 59 in the workbook.

Note: Here is a slight variation on the instructions given in the workbook. Have your students describe to themselves an uncomfortable place in their bodies which they would like to make feel better. Tell your students to select a tension image that really captures the essence of their tense or painful area. (For instance, a burning, stabbing sensation might bring to mind a sword of dry ice.) Then instruct your students to come up with an image that will greatly reduce or eliminate the tension or pain. Finally, let the two images interact so that the image of tension or pain is diminished, or gotten rid of, by the image of relief. For example, sun shining brightly on the sword of dry ice as it evaporates. Have your students share their images in groups of four or ask for examples in the large group.

3. Creating Your Special Place

Time: 10 minutes

Instructions: See pages 59 to 60 of the workbook.

Note: Tell your students that their special place may be a real place where they have experienced feeling completely relaxed and safe; or it can be a creation of their imagination. Also mention that they may see, hear, taste, smell, and feel their special place in detail, or they may just have a strong general sense of being there. What is important is that they experience and enjoy their special place in their own unique way.

4. Finding Your Inner Guide

Time: 8 minutes

Instructions: See pages 60 and 61 of the workbook.

Note: This is an optional exercise. While everybody seems to have a positive response to their special place, some people are frightened or saddened by this exercise. This latter group of individuals typically imagine guides who are dead or not to be trusted. Thus, it's a good idea not to combine the two exercises the first time that you teach Creating Your Special Place.

The value of tapping into one's inner guide cannot be underestimated. The people who have difficulties with Finding Your Inner Guide will either work them through or discontinue using this exercise.

An alternative to Finding Your Inner Guide that does not generate negative feelings is Receptive Visualization, found on page 56 of the workbook. Tell your students that they must be patient with these exercises, and may have to practice them for a while before receiving any guidance.

5. Listening to Music

Optional Instructions: See pages 61 to 62 of the workbook.

Note: Because listening to music is such an important and easy way to relax, you will want to introduce your students to various types of relaxing recorded sounds, including natural sounds. You can play music before and after class and during breaks. You can use soft background music while teaching some of the relaxation exercises or while your students are filling out questionnaires. Let your class know what you are playing and where they can purchase it. If invited, your students will quickly expand your knowledge of "relaxing sounds."

Special Notes

1. You need to reiterate to your class the three suggestions (A, B, and C) on page 62 of the workbook. The remainder of this chapter is optional.

2. Laughter is an excellent form of tension release. In addition to the humor exercise suggested on page 62 of the workbook, you may want to demonstrate the power of humor by telling a few jokes, sharing an amusing human interest story, or playing part of an audiotape of one of your favorite comics. Encourage your students to look at the humorous side of their problems.

3. A creative outlet can relieve stress and tension. Many adults put aside playing music, writing, painting, or doing crafts long ago in lieu of meeting obligations and getting ahead. The exercise, taken from *Drawing on the Right Side of the Brain,* is a good homework assignment that will demonstrate the relaxing effect of the creative process. It is described on page 63 of the workbook. Ask your students, who have a creative outlet, how it effects their tension level. Suggest to them that they take up an old creative interest, or discover a new one for themselves.

Audiotape

The New Harbinger Publications 21-minute cassette tape on "Imagination" is based on the first edition of *The Relaxation & Stress Reduction Workbook* and does not closely adhere to the chapter in the third edition. Use it to get additional ideas for Visualization exercises. Play portions of it for your students in lieu of taking them through the Visualization exercises yourself. It is divided into the following segments:

1. Introduction to Imagination as a stress reduction relaxation tool

2. Metaphorical Images

3. Change pain by pushing it away or changing its size or shape

4. Body scan for tension which is red, and relaxation which is blue; turn all to blue

5. Images of warmth for relaxation

6. Putting down the tension and stress in your life on a mountain path on the way to your special place

7. Active remembering and then letting go

8. Finding an ally

7

Self Hypnosis

Introduction

Purpose:
Self hypnosis can be used as a form of deep relaxation, using auto suggestions to enhance stress management and personal goals.

Time: 5 minutes

Instructions: See pages 65 and 66 of the workbook.

Note: Hypnosis has gotten some bad press due to "stage hypnosis" and "friendly pranks." People do not want to be made fools of, nor do anything that would harm themselves or others. It is therefore important to stress that the person experiencing a self hypnotic trance is completely in control.

Pendulum Exercise

Purpose:
Use the pendulum to ask questions of the subconscious mind.

Time:
A minimum of 20 minutes. Most people enjoy spending a great deal of time on this exercise.

Materials:
A pendulum (see workbook instructions on how to make one). For best results, the paper with the circle and cross on it should lay flat on a table, with the person seated in front of it.

Instructions:
This is an optional exercise. Your students will probably want to try it on their own at home. Have your students read pages 67 to 71 of the workbook for instructions.

Convincer Exercises

Purpose:
These are simple exercises that demonstrate to the novice that the subconscious mind, responding to simple suggestions, can take over automatic muscle movement and allow the individual to respond without conscious effort.

Time:
Each of these "convincers" take no more than 5 minutes.

Space:
Have your students stand at least an arm's length apart.

Instructions:
1. Two examples of convinces are Postural Sway and Postural Suggestion, found on page 69 of the workbook.

2. Have your students stand, then take them through these two exercises.

The Self Induction

Purpose:
The best way to introduce your students to hypnotic induction is through a demonstration in which they experience a light to medium trance.

Time: 20 minutes

Instructions:
1. As your outline, you can use Your Own Induction Talk on pages 72 and 73 of the workbook, or play the 15-minute induction on side 1 of the audiotape published by New Harbinger Publications on *Self Hypnosis*.

2. Before starting the induction, have your students select a word or phrase such as "relax now" or "peaceful, safe and warm" or anything else that has a pleasant and relaxing connotation, for example, their favorite color or place. Tell participants to use this key word or phrase when they are closing their eyes during hypnotic induction.

3. As you give the induction, speak slowly, calmly, and in a slight monotone. Remember to pause in order to give people time to respond to your instructions.

4. When you have completed the induction, return to your normal voice.

5. Suggest that participants get up and stretch. Do not do this exercise at the end of a session. Give people ample time to come out of their trance. You may want to call a five-minute break. Encourage people to get up and walk around.

6. Have people break into groups of four to discuss their experience with this exercise. Get them thinking about how they can improve your induction to fit their particular needs. Have them share what was most and least compelling about the induction for them. Have them ask any questions that come to mind. Have one person from each group report any interesting comments or questions to the large group.

7. After you have dealt with any unanswered questions, go over the key rules for a successful self induction (see page 72 of the workbook).

8. If you did not incorporate the deepening techniques described on pages 73 and 74 of the workbook, you may want to mention them here.

Abbreviated Inductions and Five Finger Exercise

Purpose:
These are mini-relaxation exercises that create feelings of calm and alertness. The Five Finger Exercise is useful for people who have low energy, are depressed, or are suffering from low self-esteem.

Time:
These inductions take less than five minutes to teach, and only moments to perform once a person becomes proficient with self hypnosis.

Instructions:
The shorthand techniques, such as the "pencil drop" described on pages 74 and 75, are optional.

Hypnotic Suggestions

Purpose:
Many symptoms of stress are a result of learned habitual responses to stress. Once in a relaxed state of mind, a person is more suggestible. This is an opportunity to suggest new ways of responding to old stresses.

Time: 15 to 30 minutes

Instructions:

1. Go over the rules for hypnotic suggestions. Then have your students write hypnotic suggestions for the 12 problems listed on page 77 of the workbook.

2. Have them compare their answers with those in the workbook on the bottom of page 77 and on page 78.

3. Have them write down at least three of their own problems and then write hypnotic suggestions for each one of them.

4. *Optional:* If you do not have time to do this exercise in class, you can suggest that your students do it as homework.

5. Whether this exercise is a class or homework assignment, you will need to give your students an opportunity to correct their errors on the hypnotic suggestions applied to their own problems. This can be done in groups of four, followed by the reporter from each group bringing up any interesting comments or questions when all groups come together.

6. As an option, you can go over the first several problems in the workbook with the class as a whole. Ask for hypnotic suggestions from class members for each of the problems. Quickly shift to asking for real problems from the class. Ask for hypnotic suggestions for each of these problems. With this option, you are able to immediately explain errors, and give some additional good examples.

7. Suggest as homework that your students write and audiotape their own self-induction, and to include one or more of the hypnotic suggestions dealing with problems they want to work on. Tell them to listen to this tape once a day for a week, and report back on their experience.

Audiotape

The New Harbinger Publications cassette tape on *Self Hypnosis* covers all the major points in the workbook chapter. Most important, it includes two inductions that demonstrate the nonverbal aspects of self-hypnosis such as tone of voice, cadence, and pauses.

Side 1, which is 27 minutes long, includes:

- Introduction to Self Hypnosis
- Exercises on Postural Sway and Postural Suggestion to demonstrate the power of suggestion
- Fifteen-minute induction
- Five rules on how to do effective inductions

Side 2, which is 30 minutes, includes:

- Four ways to deepen an induction
- Ten-minute induction, incorporating the four deepening techniques
- Abbreviated inductions
- How to create and use hypnotic suggestions

8

Autogenics

Introduction

Purpose:
Autogenic training is a systematic method of relaxation, using auto suggestion.

Time: 30 minutes

Instructions:

1. See pages 81 through 90 of the workbook.

2. Give a brief historical introduction to Autogenics.

3. Explain briefly the physiology of each of the basic six verbal formulas for physical regulation.

4. State the contraindications as well as benefits.

5. Explain and give examples of:
   - The three basic AT postures
   - Settling into a position that is comfortable for you
   - Passive concentration
   - Silent, steady repetition of the verbal formula
   - Use of visual, auditory, and tactile images to enhance the verbal formula (e.g., arms made of lead, warm sun, steady metronome or child's swing)
   - Returning to the formula when distracted
   - "Autogenic discharges"
   - Ending an AT session with "When I open my eyes I will feel refreshed and alert"
   - Make sure your students are not still in a trancelike state as you move on to their regular activities

6. Have your class practice this brief version of the first four AT verbal formulas. The fifth and sixth verbal formulas are not included for brevity's sake and because they can be problematic for certain people.

- Both of my arms are heavy.
- Both of my legs are heavy.
- My arms and legs are heavy.
- Both of my arms are warm.
- Both of my legs are warm.
- My arms and legs are warm.
- My heartbeat is calm and regular.
- It breathes me.

7. Instruct your students to say to themselves the first line four times, taking five seconds each time and pausing three seconds between each recitation. Have them do the same for each of the lines. Demonstrate the pace, using the first line.

8. You may want to give your students a typed version to refer to as they go through the formulas on their own.

9. After class members have completed this exercise, give them a five-minute break. Instruct them to get up, stretch, and walk around.

10. After the break, have students share their experiences in groups of four for five minutes, then have one person from each group report any interesting comments or questions when the large group reconvenes.

11. Suggest that they practice this brief version at home several times a day for a week.

12. Remind class participants that this is not how Autogenics is traditionally taught, and that if they are interested in approaching it more systematically, they can follow the 12-week program in the workbook or attend an Autogenics Training Workshop.

13. Once the students have mastered the basic six verbal formulas for physical regulation, they are ready to try the Meditative Exercises briefly described in the workbook on pages 88 to 90.

Audiotape

The New Harbinger Publications cassette tape on Autogenics is 37 minutes long and goes through the 12-week program described in the workbook. It would be worth your while to listen to part of it to get a sense of the pacing used for saying the verbal formulas.

9

Thought Stopping

Introduction

Purpose:
This technique eliminates nonproductive and unpleasant thoughts. It is one of the easiest stress management techniques to learn. Your students will report a high level of success with it.

Time: 25 minutes

Materials: A timer with an alarm
Rubber bands (optional)

Instructions:
1. Briefly describe this technique, its origin, and the various explanations for its success.

2. State clearly what kind of thinking it works best in eliminating: nonproductive, unrealistic, self-defeating thoughts that waste your time and make you feel bad.

3. The Stressful Thoughts Inventory on workbook pages 92 to 94 is optional. Most people know instantly what you are talking about and can identify a number of such thoughts that they would like to get rid of.

4. Follow steps two through five of thought stopping in the workbook on pages 95 and 96.

5. Suggest other types of thought substitution that work well:
   - A pleasant fantasy or memory completely unrelated to the stressful thought.
   - An activity such as whistling or singing, or getting up and walking around.

   Thought substitution can be described as "changing the radio station when you don't like what you are listening to."

6. Review the special considerations on page 97 of the workbook with your students.

7. Tell them to work on only one stressful thought at a time. It is important that they make an agreement with themselves at the onset to use thought stopping every time they catch themselves having the stressful thought.

8. Following these instructions, a stressful thought can be neutralized within a few days. This does not mean that a person will never have the stressful thought again. But it does seem to lose its power and occur much less frequently. Occasionally, a person will have to use Thought Stopping more than once on an old stressful thought that reappears.

9. Answer questions in the large group.

Audiotape

The New Harbinger cassette tape on "Thought Stopping" is twenty minutes long. It explains the technique and goes through steps 2 to 5 in the workbook. It even has varying timed intervals of silence for dwelling on the stressful thought and signals for when to stop.

10

Refuting Irrational Ideas

Introduction

Purpose:
Rational Emotive Therapy (RET) reduces stressful emotions and physiological arousal by identifying a person's irrational, extremely negative self-talk and changing it to rational, appropriate, and less extreme self-talk.

Time: One hour

Materials:
At least one copy of the homework sheet on page 114 in the workbook for each student. They can make additional copies from their workbook or from the copy that you give them.

Instructions:
1. Briefly describe the basic tenets of RET as outlined on workbook pages 100 and 101.

2. Some people take an hour or more to fill out and score the Belief Inventory on pages 101 to 105 of the workbook. Have your students do it as homework or skip it.

3. You will need this time to give a lecture including at least the first 10 of the 21 irrational ideas. Explain why they are irrational and extreme, and give examples of less extreme and more appropriate ideas for each irrational idea.

4. Conclude this lecture with the Rules to Promote Rational Thinking on page 110 of the workbook and then answer any questions.

5. Walk your students through steps A through E for Refuting Irrational Ideas in the workbook pages 110 to 114. Either go over the homework example or call for an example from students and then take the class through steps A through E again.

6. Give class members the homework assignment to spend 20 minutes a day doing this exercise, using examples from their daily lives. Suggest that they make copies of the blank homework sheet to fill in for their convenience.

7. At the beginning of the following session, have the students go over their homework in groups of four. Have them share one example of steps A through E and get corrective feedback from their particular group. Then have one member of the group report back to the large group any interesting comments or questions.

8. After you deal with unanswered questions in the large group, you may want to review the special considerations on page 115 of the workbook.

9. Tell your students to get into the habit of asking themselves, "What am I feeling?" and "What am I telling myself about this situation?" whenever they have an extremely negative emotional response to a situation. In this way, they will learn to identify their irrational self-talk, have an opportunity to mentally go through this homework assignment, and to tell themselves something less extreme and more appropriate that will generate less stressful emotions.

Rational Emotive Imagery

Purpose:
Use imagination to change excessively unpleasant emotional responses to stressful events into less intense, more appropriate emotional responses.

Time: 30 minutes.
This technique is not as complicated and time consuming to teach as Refuting Irrational Ideas. If you are pressed for time and can teach only one of the cognitive techniques, you may prefer to try this one.

Instructions:
1. Briefly go over the five steps for Rational Emotive Imagery with the class, using an example. See pages 115 and 116 of the workbook.

2. Have the class take a few minutes to get into a comfortable position and relax.

3. Take students one step at a time through the five steps again, instructing them to focus on a stressful event of their own. Give them ample time to use their imagination to transform their original response to their stressful situation to a more appropriate one.

4. When they are through, have them write down their original emotions, their new emotions, and what they changed in their belief system in order to get from one to the other.

5. Have participants share their experiences in groups of three or four. The people in the small group can offer suggestions for alternative beliefs to assist an individual who had difficulty shifting from the more extreme to the less extreme emotions. Have one person report back to the large group with any questions.

6. Go over the three levels of insight necessary to change habitual emotional responses. These insight levels are listed at the bottom of page 117 of the workbook.

7. As a homework assignment, you can suggest that your students practice Rational Emotive Imagery 20 minutes a day for a week. On page 116 of the workbook is a list of sample situations and alternative emotional responses. On the following page, you can ask your students to fill in their own stressful situations, along with their stressful and more appropriate emotions. They can use this list to practice Rational Emotive Imagery.

11

Coping Skills Training

Introduction

Purpose:
This technique allows the individual to practice responding to a stressful event in a relaxed manner, using Guided imagery, Progressive Relaxation, Deep Breathing, and Stress Coping remarks.

Time: 5 minutes

Instructions:
1. A good way to introduce this topic is to describe a few anecdotal stories of stressful situations in which people typically respond with symptoms of anxiety. Ask for a few examples from individuals in the class.

2. Explain how anxiety is a learned response to a stressful situation, and that it is possible to learn how to respond to the same situation in a relaxed manner.

3. Briefly describe how Coping Skills Training teaches greater self-control (see page 119 of the workbook).

Learning To Relax Efficiently

Introduce Coping Skills Training after your students have already mastered Progressive Relaxation and the basic breathing techniques.

Making a Stressful Events Hierarchy

Time:
This takes about 15 minutes. You may want to ask your students to do the hierarchy as homework, since some people will need much longer. Alternatively, you can have people finish their hierarchy at home.

Materials: At least two pieces of paper and pen or pencil.

Instructions: See pages 120 to 122 of the workbook.

Note: You may want to tell your students to limit their stressful situations to those they are likely to encounter often, so that they will have ample opportunity to practice their Coping Skills. Once they have mastered Coping Skills, they are likely to spontaneously apply them to infrequent stressful situations.

Applying Relaxation Techniques to Your Hierarchy

Time: 10 to 15 minutes

Instructions:
Have your students get into a comfortable position and relax, using Progressive Relaxation and Deep Breathing. Follow the instructions on pages 122 to 123 of the workbook.

Stress Coping Thoughts

Time: 15 minutes

Materials: paper and pen or pencil.

Instructions:
1. See pages 123 through 125 in workbook.

2. Give a brief lecture on the four elements of an emotional response, with emphasis on thought. Show how the feedback loop can create a vicious circle: negative thoughts to stressful physical reactions to stressful behavioral choices to more negative thoughts. Explain how Stress Coping Thoughts can create a feedback loop that leads to a sense of self-control and relaxation.

2. Go over the examples of Stress Coping Statements under each of the four categories in Meichenbaum and Cameron's stress inoculation program.

3. Have your students think of one of their stressful situations in which they would like to respond with greater self-control and relaxation. Tell them to write it at the top of their paper. Under this, have them write the first category: **Preparation.** Halfway down the page, have them write the second category: **Confronting the stressful situation.** On the other side of the paper have them write: **Coping with fear;** and halfway down the paper: **Reinforcing success.**

4. Have your students fill in Stress Coping Statements for each of the four categories appropriate for their specific stressful situation. While they can use examples from the workbook, they should come up with at least two of their own Stress Coping Statements for each category.

5. Tell your students to memorize their Stress Coping Statements and/or have this list ready to use when they are most likely to find themselves in their stressful situation. When first learning this skill, they can review these statements just before they are about to encounter their stressful situation.

6. Suggest to your students that they may want to practice using this skill with their stressful situation in front of a mirror, on video or audio recorder, or with a friend as an intermediate step before trying them out in vivo.

Coping "In Vivo"

Instructions:

Once your students have learned to respond in a relaxed manner, using progressive relaxation and deep breathing, to their stressful situations when they imagine them, and once they have memorized their stress coping statements, they are ready to apply these skills to real life situations. Some setbacks are expected. But with practice, relaxation and stress coping thoughts will become the automatic response to stressful situations and physical sensations. See the example on pages 125 to 127 in the Workbook. Here are a few suggestions for your students to help them with this phase of the training:

1. If possible, begin using the relaxation techniques before entering the stressful situation. Otherwise, use the first hint of physical or emotional distress as a cue to relax.

2. Remember to breathe. Slow, deep natural breaths are ideal, but just remembering to breathe while going through your stressful experience will help significantly.

3. At first, rehearse the coping statements just before entering the stressful situation. Keep a list of them handy.

4. Use coping statements while going through the stressful situation.

5. Afterwards, review how it went. Add coping statements to combat aspects of the stressful situation that were not previously taken into consideration. Replace ineffective old statements with more potent ones.

6. Practice these skills often to make them automatic. This is why it is important to select stressful situations that occur frequently.

12

Assertiveness Training

Introduction

Purpose:
How a person relates to others can be a significant source of stress. Assertive communication allows the individual to set limits and express what he wants, feels and believes, while taking into account the rights and feelings of others. This tends to minimize interpersonal strain.

Mini Assertiveness Course

Time:
This is a topic that can easily be expanded into a course all its own. How can you possibly teach Assertiveness Training in an hour or two? If you are pressed for time, here is a suggested outline that you can cover in an hour to an hour and a half.

Instructions:
1. *Optional:* Have your students fill in the blanks in response to the six problem situations presented on workbook pages 131 and 132. As they answer these questions, they will become more curious about assertiveness. (5 minutes)

2. Introduce Assertiveness Training (see pages 132 to 134 of the workbook). This includes a list of Mistaken Traditional Assumptions versus Your Legitimate Rights. The basic assumptions regarding your rights are summarized on the bottom of page 134 of the workbook. The list of Assumptions and Rights is optional in this abbreviated presentation because it is so time consuming (at least one-half hour). (5 to 8 minutes)

3. Define aggressive, passive, and assertive communication (see page 135 in the workbook). Test your students' ability to distinguish these three styles of interaction by asking them to label the six scenes presented on pages 136 and 137 as aggressive, passive, or assertive. A quick and fun way to do this exercise is to read aloud the first scene, ask for the correct label from a student, and then ask why he chose that particular label. If the label is incorrect, ask if someone else had another label and why they chose that label. Proceed through the other five scenes in this manner. (15 to 20 minutes)

4. *Optional:* Have your students go over their answers to the questions on pages 131 and 132 in the workbook and label their responses as aggressive, assertive or passive. Ask them if their answers tend to fall predominantly under one label? (5 minutes)

5. *Optional:* Instruct your students to fill out column A only of The Assertiveness Questionnaire on workbook pages 138 to 140. They can fill out column B at their leisure. (5 minutes)

6. Teach your students the Short Form Assertiveness Technique on pages 147 to 148 of the workbook. Note that this is the same as steps three, four, and five in Your Script Change on pages 142 to 143 of the workbook. Demonstrate the Short Form Assertiveness Technique. (10 minutes)

7. Instruct participants to write an assertive message for one of their problem areas. They can refer back to the items they checked off on The Assertiveness Questionnaire to identify a problem area. (5 minutes)

8. In groups of three, have each individual briefly state the "when," the "who," and the "what" of their problem situation, and then state their assertive message. The other group members can give constructive feedback about the assertive message. Does it include the three elements: "I think," "I feel," and "I want?" Is it clear? Is it complete? Does it avoid blame? Allow about 5 minutes per group member to present his or her problem situation and assertive message, and to receive feedback. (15 minutes)

   When you call the large group back together, ask for questions and comments. (5 to 10 minutes)

Long Form

Instructions

1. Have your students respond to the six problem situations on pages 131 to 132 of the workbook. You may choose to read the situations and have your students answer on a blank sheet of paper, to make copies of the problem situations available for your students to write on, or have your students answer these questions from their own workbooks to do at home or in class.

2. Introduce Assertiveness Training (see pages 132 to 133 of the workbook). (5 minutes)

3. Go over the Mistaken Traditional Assumptions versus Your Legitimate Rights.
   • You may choose to lecture on this topic. (30 minutes)

- You may give this as a homework assignment and then divide the class into groups of four to talk about the beliefs people held as children versus as adults. To focus discussion, ask people to comment only on those Legitimate Rights they have difficulty accepting as adults. (15 minutes)

- You can ask a class member to take a Traditional Assumption position and defend it for a minute. Then ask another student to take the position of the juxtaposed Legitimate Right and defend it for a minute. You can demonstrate how to do this, using the first Traditional Assumption and Legitimate Right in the list. Explain that this may take some play acting for people who are defending positions that they themselves do not hold. As soon as the first Traditional Assumption and Legitimate Right has been presented, move right on to the next. Take questions and comments at the end. (30 minutes)

4. Describe the Three Basic Interpersonal Styles on page 135 of the workbook.
   - Test your students' ability to distinguish these three styles using the method described earlier in the Short Form for teaching Assertiveness.

   - Have your students go over their answers to the questions on pages 131 and 132 of the workbook. Follow the instructions in the short form.

5. Tell your students to fill out the Assertiveness Questionnaire on pages 138 to 140 of the workbook. This can be done as homework or classwork. (10–15 minutes)

6. Explain and demonstrate how to do a problem scene. Have your students write out a description of two to four of their problem scenes, using the instructions on pages 140 to 142 of the workbook.
   - This can be done as homework or class work.

   - Have students break into groups of four in which each person presents one example of a problem scene and the other three give constructive feedback. You may want to have people underscore the criteria for a good problem scene on the bottom of page 140 and the top of page 141, or write these criteria on a blackboard for the small groups to refer to. Have one person report back any interesting comments or unanswered questions when the large group reconvenes. (30 minutes)

7. "Your Script for Change"
   - Instructions: See pages 142 to 147 in the workbook.

   - Go over the six steps in the "LADDER."

   - Explain the difference between a poor and good LADDER by using examples.

   - Have individuals write an example of a LADDER based on one of their problem scenes.

- Break the large group into groups of four, and have each individual present his LADDER and get constructive feedback from the other three people.

- Have a spokesman from each of the small groups bring any interesting comments or questions back to the large group. This is an important opportunity for you to correct any major misconceptions.

- Demonstrate how to use the LADDER in a role play between yourself and a class volunteer, or set up a role play between two students, using one of their LADDER scripts.

- Mention the five basic rules for assertive body language.

- Have each individual in the same small groups role play their LADDER with one other person, while the other two members observe and then give feedback. The other person in the role play can give valuable information about what it was like to be on the receiving end of the LADDER.

- Have a spokesman from each of the small groups bring any interesting questions or comments back to the large group.

- Mention to the group that the LADDER is a valuable tool to use when a person is faced with a major problem scene that he can anticipate, such as asking his boss for a raise or setting limits with a friend. It is also good to use in problem scenes where the individual has a long established pattern of responding nonassertively. In such cases, he can anticipate the problem coming up again, and can think through and rehearse his new assertive response.

- Have your students practice this technique as homework at least twice. (75 minutes)

8. Short Form Assertive Technique
   - Instructions: See pages 147 and 148.

   - Point out to your students that the Short Form Assertive Technique is identical to three of the elements in "Your Script for Change":

     "Define the problem" is the same as "I think,"
     "Describe your feelings" is the same as "I feel,"
     "Express your request" is the same as "I want."

   - Demonstrate this technique to the class in a role play, and then have your students practice in groups of four.

   - Have your students practice this technique as homework. (30 to 40 minutes)

9. Learning How To Listen
   - Instructions: See workbook pages 149 to 151.

   - Explain assertive listening.

   - Demonstrate assertive listening in a role play.

   - Have students break into groups of four to role play assertive listening. The person who is listening should request the speaker to play the role of someone that the listener would have difficulty listening to in real life.

   - Have the spokesman from each small group report back to the large group any interesting comments, problems or questions.

   - Have your students practice this technique as homework.
     (30 to 40 minutes)

10. Arriving at a Workable Compromise
    - Instructions: See pages 151 to 152 in the workbook.

    - Explain Workable Compromise.

    - Demonstrate Workable Compromise.

    - Have your students go back to their problem scenes of their LADDER and think about the best way for them to arrive at a Workable Compromise for each one of these scenes.

    - Have your students role play Workable Compromise with one other person, with two people observing and coaching.

    - Have your students practice this technique as homework.
      (30 to 40 minutes)

11. Avoiding Manipulation

    - Instructions: See pages 152 to 154 in the workbook.

    - Explain each of the seven techniques for dealing with manipulation, giving a brief demonstration of each as you go.

    - Mention that two of the dangers in using Content-to-Process Shift are inaccurately reading the other person's mind and appearing condescending.

    - Point out that Defusing and Assertive Delay are basically other ways of saying "time out" when you realize the conversation is going nowhere.

    - Note that Assertive Agreement, Clouding, and Assertive Inquiry are three ways of dealing with critics.

    - Go over the typical blocking gambits that are used to block assertive requests. Give examples of each and of how to deal assertively with each.

• If you decide to have your students take the time to practice any of these techniques in class, the Broken Record and the techniques for dealing with criticism are the most important.
(at least 15 minutes)

Special Note

When you have four to five hours, you can teach everything in the *Assertiveness Training* chapter in the workbook. Ideally, you should have at least twice that much time, spread out over four to eight weeks. Assertive behavior change involves interacting with significant people in an individual's life. It is helpful when the person can practice an assertive technique during role play in class, and follow this up with an "in vivo" homework assignment. He then can return to the next class session to report on and fine tune his newly acquired assertive skill. It is also useful when the individual can read and reflect on the Mistaken Traditional Assumptions versus Your Legitimate Rights so that he is more conscious of what he believes, why he believes as he does, and how this affects his behavior. Finally, it saves class time when students can fill out some of the questionnaires as homework, to be discussed in a later class.

13

Time Management

Introduction

Purpose:
The people attending Stress Management classes typically feel overwhelmed with responsibilities which they have too little time to fulfill. When will they find the time to relax and enjoy themselves, let alone time to do the Stress Management homework assignments? Time Management suggests ways to simplify one's life by choosing to do only what is really important, and to eliminate low-priority activities.

Instructions: See page 155 of the workbook.

Time: 2 minutes

Time Inventory

Time:
If given as a homework assignment, it will take about 15 minutes a day, plus 10 to 15 minutes to tabulate the amount of time spent on specific activities during an average day. If done in class from memory, it will take 15 minutes.

Material: three pieces of paper and pen or pencil.

Instructions: See pages 156 to 159 of the workbook.
1. *Optional:* For the purpose of comparing current schedules with goals, it is sufficient to do this exercise from memory. If done from memory, have your students fill out a time inventory for one typical week day and one typical week-end day.

2. Ask your students to look at their own inventories and consider how they might want to change how they are currently spending their time.

Setting Priorities

Time: 30 to 60 minutes

Materials: 3 pieces of paper and a pen or pencil.

Instructions: See pages 159 to 161 in the workbook.

1. *Optional:* To loosen up your students' imagination, have them do the following relaxation fantasy exercise: Tell them to get into a comfortable position and take several slow, relaxing deep breaths. Then have them go through their body, using Progressive Relaxation. Finally have them return to their breathing for a couple of minutes, and do a breathing exercise of their choice. This will take no more than 10 minutes.

   While they are still in their relaxed state, with their eyes closed, ask them to imagine themselves toward the end of their life, sitting comfortably and reflecting back over their life. Have them ask themselves: "What have I done or experienced that I am particularly pleased or proud of?" After a pause for them to reflect, have them ask themselves, "What do I regret?"

   Ask them to let this fantasy fade and another to take its place: "Imagine that you have just been to see your doctor who has informed you that you have just one year before you die suddenly without any prior outward signs of illness. Imagine how you would spend that next and last year of your life?"

   Instruct participants to let go of this fantasy, and when they open their eyes to write down what came to mind as important to experience or do when they imagined themselves at the end of their life and then when they imagined themselves with only one year to live. (20 to 30 minutes)

2. You can follow the instructions in the workbook under Setting Priorities for writing goals, prioritizing them, and finally selecting which goals to work on now. (30 minutes)

Breaking Priorities Down Into Manageable Steps

Purpose:
Often people hesitate to tackle a new goal because it seems so complex, so much work, or so far away. For these reasons, it is important to carefully break down a goal into manageable steps.

Time: 20 minutes

Materials: paper, pen, and list of personal goals.

Instructions: See pages 161 to 162 of the workbook.
1. First explain and then demonstrate how to break down a goal into manageable steps, using an example of your own.

2. Have your students write the steps for one of their goals and then go over these steps in a group of four, so that they can get feedback and suggestions.

3. Answer questions when the large group reconvenes.

4. As a homework assignment, have your students go through this exercise with their own goals.

Making Time

Time: 5 minutes

Instructions: See pages 162 and 163 in the workbook.
1. *Optional:* Read these rules aloud.

2. Encourage your students to read this section on their own and plan ways to integrate these rules into their lives.

3. *Optional:* Ask your students for additional ways that they have successfully made time for themselves.

Making Decisions

Materials: paper and pen

Time: 30 minutes

Instructions: See pages 163 to 165 in the workbook.
1. This is an optional exercise. It is useful for procrastinators and anyone who has difficulty making decisions.

2. Explain and demonstrate how to do this exercise, using an example of your own.

3. Have your students write an example of their own.

4. Instruct your students to share their example with a group of three others who can give them feedback and suggestions.

5. Have a reporter from each of the small groups report back to the big group any interesting comments or questions.

Rules for Overcoming Procrastination

Time: 5 minutes

Instructions: See pages 164 to 165 in the workbook.
1. This is an optional exercise.

2. You may choose to read this list to the class, or suggest that your students read it on their own.

14

Job Stress Management

Introduction

Purpose:
Even if most of the people in your class are housewives or full-time students, they may be suffering from the burnout that comes from chronically not feeling in control of their lives. They would benefit, therefore, from tools designed to empower them. This is the central theme of Job Stress Management.

Time: 5 minutes

Instructions: See pages 167 and 168 of the workbook.

Ten Steps Toward Managing Your Job Stress

Step 1. Identify Your Symptoms of Job Stress

Time: 8 minutes

Materials:
If this is done as class work, you may choose to make copies of the inventory for people to fill out, read the questions and have them write their answers on a blank piece of paper, or have them read the questions from the book.

Instructions: See pages 168 and 169 in the workbook.

Step 2: Identify the Sources of Your Job Stress

Time: 10 minutes

Materials:
Either have your students use their own workbook or give them copies of this inventory along with a blank piece of paper for their answers.

Instructions: See pages 169 to 172 of the workbook.

Step 3: Identify How You Respond to Your Specific Job Stressors

Time: 40 minutes

Materials: paper and pen

Instructions: See pages 172 to 175 of the workbook.

Note:
- This is a good homework assignment. Students may want to take notes during their work day or at the end of the day.

- Have students review their response to stressors in groups of four.

- Answer questions.

Step 4: Set Goals to Respond More Effectively to Your Job Stressors

Time: 30 minutes

Materials: piece of paper and pen.

Instructions:
1. See pages 175 to 177 in the workbook.

2. Give your students 10 to 15 minutes to write a contract.

3. Have students review their contracts in groups of four for 10 to 15 minutes.

4. Answer questions when the large group reconvenes.

Step 5: Motivate Yourself

Time: 5 minutes

Materials: paper and pen

Instructions:
1. See pages 177 to 178 of the workbook.

2. Have your students write several ways that they can reward themselves for working on and achieving their goals.

3. Tell your students to write a more preferred activity that they can use to motivate themselves to do a less preferred activity.

Step 6: Change Your Thinking

Time: one hour

Materials: paper and pen

Instructions:

1. See pages 178 to 180 in the workbook.

2. After you have explained the three generic thoughts about work that trigger painful emotions, have your students write examples of each from their own lives on a piece of paper.

3. After you have explained how to cope with the first stressful generic thought, have your students write coping statements for each of their stressful thoughts that fall in this category. Then answer any questions.

4. After you have explained how to change or adapt to work stressors, have your students write how they will do this for each of the statements they wrote under this category. Then answer any questions.

5. After you have suggested that class members consider their options and the risk of pursuing these options, have them write options and risks involved for each thought they listed under the third category. Then answer any questions.

6. Have your students meet in groups of four and share one generic thought and its coping statement from each of the three categories. Answer questions when the large group reconvenes.

Step 7: Deal With Your Boss

Time: 30 minutes

Materials: paper and pen

Instructions:

1. See pages 180 to 182 of the workbook.

2. Have your students write answers to the six questions beginning on the bottom of workbook page 180. Suggest that a good time to talk with their boss is at the time of their annual review. If that is a long way off, they can set up a special time to talk with him or her.

3. After you have explained why it is important to understand what motivates bosses, have your students write responses to the three statements on the bottom of page 181 of the workbook. Then have your students share their answers with four others and also get feedback and suggestions.

Step 8: When in Conflict, Negotiate

Time: 45 to 60 minutes

Materials: paper and pen

Instructions:
1. See pages 182 to 183 in workbook.

2. Explain and demonstrate, using role playing, the four steps of negotiation.

3. Have your students write a script to negotiate an office conflict, using this four-part model.

4. Divide your class into groups of four. Let each person take a turn at role playing their script with one other person in the small group. The two observers can act as coaches. At the end of the role play, have the small group discuss what was good about it, as well as what could be improved.

5. Have the small group reporter share any interesting comments and ask questions when the large group reconvenes. Answer any questions.

Step 9. Pace and Balance Yourself

Time: 15 minutes

Materials: paper and pen

Instructions:
1. See pages 183 and 189 in the workbook.

Additional points

2. Have your students read this section, and then write specifically how they could apply each of the eight suggestions to their lives. If an item does not apply, have them write N/A. This can be done as a homework assignment.

3. Have them share their answers in groups of four.

4. Suggest that they apply these ideas to their daily schedule.

Step 10. Know When To Quit

Time:
Guided fantasy, plus writing: 25 minutes. Writing fear and goal statements: 10 to 15 minutes. Group interaction: 20 minutes.

Materials: paper and pen

Instructions:

1. See pages 184 to 186 of the workbook.

2. *Optional:* Have your students get into a comfortable position. Lead them in a five-minute relaxation exercise.

   After they have relaxed, suggest that they imagine themselves in their current job five years from now without anything substantially changed about their job. Ask them: "What do you see . . . hear . . . feel? Are you happy? Are you doing what you want? Are you where you want to be? Let that image go for now."

   Ask them: "What would it take to make your current job more enjoyable or satisfactory? Imagine your job with these changes. What would it take to make these changes happen? Let that image go for now."

   Ask them: "Describe your ideal job. Include your job title, your job responsibilities, your boss, your co-workers, your environment, and the management."

   Tell them: "When you open your eyes, write down how you imagine it will be for you in your job in five years with no changes. Then write down what changes you think would make your current job better for you, and what it would take to make these changes happen. Finally, describe your ideal job."

3. Have them write down their fears about leaving their job. Then tell them to turn these "fear statements" into goals designed to get around the barrier. Give an example of this. Have them share a couple of fear and goal statements in groups of four for the purpose of receiving feedback. Have the small group reporters share any interesting comments or questions when the large group reconvenes.

15

Brief Combination Techniques

Introduction

Purpose:
Therapists have found that many of the techniques already presented have a more profound effect when combined.

Instructions:
1. See pages 187 to 193 in workbook.
2. Self-explanatory

Special Notes

While all of these exercises can be used for relaxation, the following are a few suggestions as to other purposes they can serve.

- Exercises for quick relaxation:
  1. Stretch and Relax
  2. Autogenic Breathing

- Exercises for thought stopping:
  3. Stop and Breathe
  4. Changing Channels

- Exercises to enhance self-esteem and mood:
  5. I Am Grateful
  8. Breath Counting
  10. Accepting Yourself

- Exercises to enhance sense of self-control:
  6. Deep Affirmation
  9. Taking Control

- Exercises to reduce pain and tension:
  7. The Tension Cutter

16

Recording Your Own Relaxation Tape

Introduction

Purpose:
To explain and demonstrate how students can make relaxation tapes tailored to their own particular needs.

Time: 30 to 40 minutes

Instructions:
1. See pages 196 to 201 in the workbook.
2. Self-explanatory
3. This is an optional topic
4. Demonstrate how you record your voice as you take your students through a relaxation exercise. You may choose to use part of the Relaxation Script in the workbook. At the end of the relaxation exercise, be sure to suggest that when they open their eyes and return to the room they will feel relaxed, refreshed, and alert. When they open their eyes, encourage them to stretch and move around. You may want to schedule a 5-minute break, go over homework, or call for questions and comments.

5. Play back a short section of what you recorded. Ask class members what they think are the ingredients of a good relaxation audiotape. Follow this discussion with any additional suggestions that have not been covered.

17

Biofeedback

Introduction

Purpose:
To show how biofeedback brings to conscious awareness subtle biological processes for the purpose of self-regulation and relaxation.

Time: 20 to 40 minutes.

Instructions:
1. See workbook pages 204 to 210.

2. Self-explanatory.

3. This is an optional topic.

4. Describe the basic principles of biofeedback and the basic types of biofeedback used for relaxation training. Point out a few examples of how a person can be aware of biofeedback without the aid of a machine: pulse, skin temperature, and sweat.

5. If possible, bring in biofeedback equipment and demonstrate its use during a relaxation exercise.

Special Notes

The great majority of people learn to relax, using the relaxation techniques already presented. A small number of people, however, fail to alleviate a symptom of tension despite using standard relaxation techniques. These people may very well benefit from biofeedback training, in addition to learning relaxation techniques.

Some people believe that they can become even more relaxed with biofeedback training. Others do not trust their abilities to relax on their own, and believe that a machine might help. For these individuals, it is particularly important to hear the merits and limitations of biofeedback.

18

Nutrition

Highlights on Nutrition for Stress Management

Purpose:
To convey the message that proper dietary habits are an integral part of a stress management program.

Time: About 30 minutes

Instructions:

1. See pages 211 through 223 of the workbook.

2. You can have your students fill out the Food Diary as homework, or take 5 to 10 minutes of class time to estimate their average servings per day.

3. Briefly go over the ten steps to good nutrition.

4. Mention that people who suffer from fatigue, moodiness, or compulsive eating should look carefully at their sugar intake.

5. Point out that while it is tempting to use alcohol to relax, it is a depressant and disturbs normal sleep patterns.

6. Stress the importance of eliminating caffeine from their diet if they have symptoms of anxiety, tension, or insomnia. This one change can bring dramatic results.

7. Unless you are an expert, do not get into a technical discussion on vitamins and mineral supplements. Suggest that your students go to their local health food store or library for information. Unfortunately, their doctor is likely not to be a good resource on this subject.

8. Divide the class into groups of four to discuss how each individual might improve his or her eating habits. Have a reporter from each small group share any interesting comments or questions when the large group reconvenes. (15 minutes in small groups)

9. If you have a relatively small class of ten or less people, you may want to informally present the information on nutrition. After the students have determined their daily average servings on the Food Diary, go around the room and ask each person how he could improve his eating habits. Inject information regarding nutrition as you interact with each student. (3 to 8 minutes per student)

19

Exercise

Basic Concepts About Exercise and Stress Management

Purpose:
To convey the message that Exercise is an important part of a stress management program.

Time: 5 to 10 minutes

Instructions:
1. See pages 225 to 227 in the workbook.

2. Briefly review the importance of exercise, especially aerobic exercise. Most people know that exercise is good for them, yet many find endless excuses not to do it. The purpose of discussing exercise is to motivate people to get involved in a regular exercise program.

3. Ask for a show of hands of people who are already engaged in a regular exercise program that includes at least 20 minutes of aerobic exercise at the minimum of three times a week. Ask these people with their hands up to leave them up if they also stretch and warm up before starting and stretch and cool down afterwards. Explain the importance of warming up and cooling down. If you have time, ask these individuals what their exercise program is.

Exercise Diary

Time: 30 minutes

Materials: paper and pen

Instructions: See pages 227 to 231 of the workbook.

Notes:
1. This is an optional exercise. It is useful for people who are currently not engaged in an exercise program and who need to overcome their excuses.

2. This exercise should be done as homework.

3. For many people, it is enough just to go over the example in the book during class to get the point.

30- to 50-Minute Exercise Program

Space Requirement: Ideally this exercise should be done in the open air on a lawn, with ample room for every student to move without coming in contact with someone else. It also can be done in a well ventilated room.

Instructions:
1. See pages 232 to 239 in the workbook.

2. This is an optional exercise.

Notes:
- Ideally, have your class meet at or go to an open area, such as a park, to go through this program. Have your students wear comfortable, loose fitting workout clothes.
- Do the minimum number of repetitions suggested, for the purpose of demonstration and to avoid over-heating people in a room.

3. Caution people not to do exercises that would aggravate any known physical problem that they have, such as a back injury, and not to do any exercise to the point that significant pain is experienced.

Establishing Goals

Time: 5 minutes

Materials: paper and pen

Instructions:
1. See pages 239 to 240 in the workbook.

2. Have your students write an exercise program tailored to their own current exercise level, interests, time, and resources.

3. Suggest that they set a two-week goal to stick to this exercise program.

4. Tell students to keep track of their exercise on a exercise log such as the one on page 240, or on a calendar that they look at daily.

Keeping at It

Time: 3 minutes

Instructions:

1. See page 240 in the workbook.

2. These points naturally flow at the end of Establishing Goals.

To Avoid Injury

Time: 3 minutes

Instructions:

1. See pages 240 to 241 of the workbook.

2. Since people's minds tend to go numb when they hear a lecture on safety, you may prefer to weave these points into your introduction or during the 30-50 Minute Exercise Program.

3. Another option is to ask your students what safety precautions they take and why.

4. A few tales of mishaps as a result of pushing the limits will be remembered better than a list of common sense rules about safety.

20

When It Doesn't Come Easy — Getting Unstuck

Introduction

Purpose:
To explore why some people are not doing the homework, not applying stress management and relaxation techniques to their daily lives, or not experiencing symptomatic relief.

Instructions:

1. See pages 243 to 247 in the workbook.

2. This topic is optional.

3. Briefly present, in lecture form, the major points in this chapter. You may choose to have your students read the workbook chapter as homework before your lecture.

4. Have your students discuss, in small groups of four, how some of the ideas presented in this chapter might apply to their situation and what they might do to change.

5. Take questions and comments when the large group reconvenes.

Special Notes

The danger of this chapter is that it places the responsibility for change and symptomatic relief on the individual. This can motivate the individual to initiate change from within, rather than wait for a miracle from without. Or it can make a person feel guilty or resigned if he is still unable to relieve his symptoms after significant effort.

It is important for the individual to be patient and to practice these techniques before deciding whether they are beneficial. If symptoms persist after a sincere effort, the individual should seek professional one-on-one help.

21

Homework

Objective

Homework is an essential part of a stress management class or workshop. It is important because:

1. It allows the student to integrate intellectual concepts and techniques into his experience.

2. Only then can the student decide which concepts and techniques are useful to him, and which are not.

3. Through repetition, a new behavior that was at first awkward will begin to feel natural.

4. If the student repeatedly experiences positive feedback in practicing a new behavior, he is likely to continue doing it long after the stress class is over.

Motivation

A major task of the stress management and relaxation instructor is to motivate students to do their homework. In a sense, class time can be looked upon as the time when students come in to get their new homework assignment and report the results of their efforts on the previous assignment. The instructor can enhance homework compliance by

- explaining the purpose of an assignment;

- describing the homework in simple step-by-step instruction orally and in writing;

- demonstrating the homework;

- giving the students an opportunity to practice any new technique in class and to ask questions before practicing it at home;

- suggesting a minimum expectation for performance, with the understanding that the students can exceed this;

- having students keep a written record of their homework progress, along with any comments and questions; and

- providing time at the beginning of the next session to discuss the homework experience and to ask questions.

Reviewing Assignments

Discussion of the previous week's homework assignment shouldn't take more than 20 minutes. In a relatively small group of eight or less students, the instructor may choose to go around and briefly check with each student on his homework experience. Or the instructor may prefer to save time and encourage group interaction by using the small group format to discuss the homework. Certainly in larger groups, small group feedback is the most efficient way to discuss homework as well as class assignments. An added bonus of using small groups is that everyone will get an opportunity to speak, including those who are shy.

When you opt for the small discussion groups, you need to provide a clear outline of questions to keep the conversation on track. You may also want to give your students these questions in writing. This is particularly useful for people who arrive late. Typical questions include:

1. Did you meet the minimum expectations of the assignment? Did you exceed the minimum expectations?

2. Do you have any questions about the instructions or your experience?

For those who did the assignment:

3. What did you learn from doing this assignment?

4. What did you like and dislike about the assignment?

5. Do you think that you would benefit from continued practice of the ideas and/or techniques you learned in this assignment? Will you continue to practice them?

For those who did not do the assignment:

6. Briefly, why did you not do the assignment? If something else took priority over your homework, what does that mean to you? Is that something that you want to change? If "yes," how can you make the change?

7. Recall why you are here. Do you think that the homework assignment might help you achieve your purpose for being here?

8. Do you want to do this homework assignment this week? If so, what would you decide to do differently this week?

"No" to Homework

It is important for a person to understand why he does not do his homework assignment, since the reasons he gives will tend to reflect how he maintains his stress patterns.

1. If he rarely says "no" to others, he is devoting most of his energy to others and has little time for himself and stress management homework assignments. He would benefit from the workbook chapters on Assertiveness Training and Time Management.

2. If he is a perfectionist, he is likely to set high standards for himself, which he cannot possibly achieve. He may respond to his high standards by not trying, criticizing himself, procrastinating until the last minute, or doing the assignment but not feeling satisfied with his results and not feeling motivated to continue doing the technique beyond the homework assignment. He needs encouragement to set reasonable goals and permission to make mistakes. He would benefit from the workbook chapters on Refuting Irrational Ideas and Time Management.

3. If he is an enthusiastic idealist who jumps into the assignment with both feet, he is likely to soon discover that doing the assignment does not net him the instant rewards hoped for. In fact, by practicing a new behavior excessively, he may create new stress in his life. Disillusioned, he loses interest, and stops. Such is the case with people who go on rigid diets or exercise programs. He needs to be reminded that to keep balance in his life he must do all things in moderation and be patient. Progress can be slow. While he needs to work steadily, the rewards will not always materialize as quickly as he would like. He would benefit from the Refuting Irrational Ideas and Time Management chapters in the workbook.

4. If he is afraid of new experiences, he will tend to interpret any minor problem as a major obstacle that he cannot overcome. Therefore, he is likely to abandon the exercise. If he becomes anxious or has a stressful thought in the middle of a relaxation exercise, he may asume that it is the fault of the exercise. He needs reassurance from the group leader that he is doing the exercises correctly and that the experiences he is having are normal. He also needs permission to be creative in solving little problems that come up in doing the homework. He would benefit from the Refuting Irrational Ideas and Coping Skills chapters in the workbook.

5. If he believes that self-improvement should not involve effort and inconvenience, he is likely to do the class assignments—but not the homework. He needs to be reminded that his old habits took a long time to form, and it stands to reason that he will have to practice a new behavior for a long time

before it becomes habitual and natural. In the meantime, new behavior is going to feel awkward, if not downright uncomfortable. Just because a person knows that exercise is good for him does not mean that he will enjoy exercising at first. Only after he has established an exercise pattern in which he can experience its benefits (e.g., improved mood, concentration, physical fitness and energy) will he be motivated to continue exercising on his own.

6. If he resents being told to do something by anyone, he is likely to resist doing homework assignments. This is a pattern that was probably established early in life, and is unlikely to change in a stress class. As a group leader, take the position that you are responsible for presenting the material, and he can do whatever he likes with it. He is responsible for his own decisions about how he uses his time. If you have good rapport with someone who is oppositional, it is sometimes fun to predict that he won't do the assignment and then be amazed when he does it to spite you. Suggest to people who do not do their assignments and appear not to be improving that one of their options is individual psychotherapy to explore their motivation. Another option is to remind them of their right to stay the same.

7. If he does the homework assignment in a manner that varies significantly from the original instructions, first determine if the general goal of the assignment was accomplished. If so, compliment him on his creativity and ability to shape the assignment to his own needs. If the general goal of the homework was not reached, point this out and ask him if he is interested in achieving this goal or satisfied with his outcome. If he wants to achieve this goal, have him meet with you or one of the students who was successful with the assignment during the break to go over the instructions and correct his misconceptions.

Here are some additional suggestions for reviewing homework assignments:
• Do not chastise people for not doing their homework. Everybody learns in different ways. Keep in mind that some people will go through the entire class without doing homework and yet appear to benefit from the class. They seem to pick up what they need by attending the class and possibly reading the book.

• When someone is conscientiously doing the assignments and yet continues to have significant symptoms of stress, he should be referred for medical and/or psychiatric evaluation.

• In further structuring the small groups, suggest that the people who did not do the assignment report after the people who did do the assignment. This ensures that those who put out the effort to do homework get corrective feedback.

- While it is useful for the individual to understand why he did not do his homework, this should not become the major focus of small group discussion. A person can simply acknowledge to the group that it was his decision not to do the assignment, why he gave priority to something else, and whether this is indicative of a pattern in his life that he could change if he wanted to. Remind people to change "I couldn't . . . " to "I chose not to . . . " Then he can decide if he wants to do the assignment during the next week, given his personal needs and priorities.

- Ask one person to volunteer to act as a spokesperson for the small group when the large group reconvenes. This person can share with the large group any interesting comments or unanswered questions that came up in the small group.

- Model clearly defined boundaries. Tell your students that you are their stress management and relaxation consultant who will share the most current concepts and techniques available to help them with their stress management problems. Remind students that they are ultimately responsible for their own well-being. You respect their right to do as they choose with their life, including the decision to remain the same by not doing anything differently. Part of your own personal stress management is not to take responsibility for decisions that are the responsibility of others.

Class Formats of Varying Lengths

One Three-Hour Presentation

I. *Introduction* (20 minutes)

    A. See Chapter 1 of workbook: "How You React to Stress"

    B. What is Stress?

    C. Three Major Sources of Stress

    D. The Fight or Flight Response

    E. Chronic Stress and Disease

    F. Typical symptoms of stress in everyday life

    G. The remainder of this presentation will focus on ways that the average person can gain greater control over the stress in his life.

II. *Take care of your playing piece in the game of life*

    A. Why is it important to take care of your body?

    It is true that your susceptibility to life-threatening illness is largely determined by your ancestry. But while you had no control over who your parents were, you do have some choice about what you do with the body you inherited. Most people who take good care of their bodies say they do so because it makes them feel good and enhances their quality of life. It also makes it easier for them to cope with the daily onslaught of stresses that can slowly wear down a body that is not kept in good condition.

    B. Exercise (5 minutes)

       1. See Chapter 19 of the workbook.

       2. Emphasize the importance of regular aerobic exercise for a minimum of 20 minutes, three times a week.

       3. Make the point that people need to create an exercise program, taking into account their current condition, their tastes, and their personality type. They must choose a form of exercise they like and to do it in a way that will be positively reinforced.

C. Nutrition (5 minutes)

    1. See Chapter 18 of the workbook.

    2. Stress the points highlighted in this guide in Chapter 18.

D. Relaxation (20 minutes)

    1. The Relaxation Response (see page 4 of the workbook).

    2. Teach The Relaxing Sigh (see page 30 of the workbook).

    3. Have your participants get into a comfortable position in their chairs. Tell them to take everything off their laps, and then teach Breathing Awareness and Deep Breathing (see pages 29 and 30 of the workbook, and Chapter 4 in this guide). Alternatively, teach Progressive Relaxation.

    4. While your participants are still in their relaxed position, have them imagine themselves in their special place (see Creating Your Special Place on pages 59 and 60 of the workbook).

    5. Toward the end of this exercise, have them describe to themselves in one brief sentence how they feel in their special place. For instance, "I am warm and relaxed, safe, and at peace."

    6. At the end of this exercise, suggest that they now return to the room relaxed, alert and refreshed. Suggest they practice, on a daily basis, the relaxation exercises they just learned, as well as carry out their plans to improve their exercise and nutrition programs.

    7. Suggest that people stand up, stretch, walk around, and take a 5-minute break.

    8. After the break, answer questions. (5 minutes)

III. *Take an active stance in shaping your environment*

A. Ten steps to effective time management drawn from Chapter 13 of the workbook (40 minutes)

    1. List your one-month, one-year, and lifetime goals.

    2. Write down how much time you spend at each kind of activity you do during the course of a typical day. For example: 8 hours sleeping, 2 hours commuting, 2 hours preparing and eating food, 2 hours watching TV, one hour on the phone talking to friends, one hour talking to mate, 8 hours working, 10 minutes daydreaming, 15 minutes in the shower, 15 minutes dressing, and 30 minutes shopping.

    3. Compare your current use of time to your important goals. Assign top, medium or low priority to all of your activities and goals.

4. Eliminate low priority items, give minimum amounts of time required to medium-level priorities, and set aside specific time to work on high priority items.

5. Allow yourself to do low priority items only when you have spent your allotted time on the high and medium priority items.

6. Break down high priority goals into manageable steps.

7. At the beginning of the day, make a list of what you plan to accomplish. Review the list at the end of the day. This is an excellent way to learn how much time specific activities really take. Unfinished tasks can be added to the next day's list, or prioritized downward.

8. Learn to say, "no."

9. Avoid rushing by scheduling ample time for each task you plan to do. Include time for interruptions and unforeseen problems.

10. Set aside several periods each day for quiet time. Arrange not to be interrupted, and focus on a deep relaxation exercise.

B. Three easy steps to setting limits and asking for what you want (30 minutes) See Short Form Assertiveness Technique on pages 147 and 148, Chapter 12, in the workbook.

IV. *Take charge of your thoughts* (30 minutes)

A. Explain how "man is not disturbed by events, but by the view he takes of them." See pages 99 and 100 in the workbook.

B. Use the exercise, Change Your Thinking, on pages 178 to 180 of the workbook to show how to alter three typical irrational beliefs.

V. *Summarize your major points and answer questions* (10 minutes)

One-Hour Presentation

This three-hour format can be shortened to a one-hour presentation as follows:

I. *Introduction remains the same* (15 to 20 minutes)

II. *Your body: make the most of what you have*

A. Summarize your points about exercise and nutrition in five minutes.

B. Do a ten-minute relaxation exercise of your choice.

III. *Take an active stance in shaping your environment*

A. Summarize the Ten Steps to Effective Time Management in ten minutes. An alternative to this is to go over the rules for Making Time on pages 162 and 163 of the workbook.

B. Summarize the "Three easy steps to setting limits and asking for what you want" in five minutes.

IV. *Take charge of your Thoughts*

A. Summarize how "Man is not disturbed by events, but by the view he takes of them" in five minutes.

B. Summarize rational alternatives to the three typical irrational beliefs in five minutes.

Save five to ten minutes at the end to summarize your major points and answer questions.

Ten-Week Class

All of the topics in *The Relaxation & Stress Reduction Workbook* can be covered in a ten-week class, allowing two hours per class. As a general rule of thumb, teach one relaxation exercise and one stress management technique each week. Begin every session, except the first one, by reviewing the preceding week's homework. It is best to do the relaxation exercise next, followed by a short break. You want your participants to be alert when they go home, especially if you are doing a night class. Do an energizing breathing exercise when you sense minds are drifting.

The following is a suggested ten-week Relaxation and Stress Reduction Class format:

Week:	Relaxation Exercise	Stress Management Technique
1	Body Awareness	Introduction
2	Breathing	Nutrition & Exercise
3	Visualization	Thought Stopping
4	Progressive Relaxation	Refuting Irrational Ideas
5	Autogenics	Coping Skills
6	Biofeedback	Time Management

7	Self Hypnosis	Assertiveness Training
8	Meditation	Job Stress Management
9	Brief Combinations	Record Own Relaxation Tape
10	Combine in a review	When It Doesn't Come Easy

12 Hour-Workshop in Two Days

Day 1

I.   *Introduction* (1¼ hours)

   A.   Simplify your life and have your students purchase the text, *The Relaxation & Stress Reduction Workbook,* as part of the price of your workshop.

   B.   See Chapter 1 of the workbook: "How You React to Stress" and Chapter 1 of this guide: "Introduction."

   C.   Introduce yourself, describing your background, especially as it relates to stress management, and why you are teaching this workshop.

   D.   Hand out an outline of your workshop, listing topics to be covered and when people can expect breaks.

   E.   Define stress.

   F.   Describe the three major sources of stress.

   G.   Explain the "Fight or Flight" Response.

   H.   Explain the relationship between chronic stress and disease.

   I.   Exercise: Schedule of Recent Experience (30 minutes)
        See pages 4 to 8 in the workbook and see Chapter 1 in this guide.

   J.   Describe typical symptoms of stress in everyday life.

   K.   Exercise: Symptoms Checklist (10 minutes)
        See pages 10 to 11 in the workbook.

   L.   Point out that the major purpose of this workshop is to teach techniques for deep relaxation and effective stress management. The benefits of these techniques will only be experienced if your students are willing to practice them regularly once the workshop is over.

(15-minute break)

II. *Take care of your playing piece in the game of life* (1½ hours)

   A.   Why is it important to take care of your body?

    1. Nature versus nurture issue
        2. Taking control of what you can
        3. Quality of life
        4. Better prepared to cope with adversity as well as normal aging.

  B. Exercise (30 minutes)

    1. See Chapter 19 in the workbook and Chapter 19 in this guide.

    2. Describe the basic forms of exercise, underscoring the health benefits of regular aerobic exercise for a minimum of 20 minutes, three times a week. Also point out the value of gradualism, warming up and cooling off, and stretching.

    3. Exercise: Have your students write their current exercise pattern. (5 minutes)

    4. Exercise: Have your students write two-week exercise goals and suggest that they keep a log of their progress. Have them also write how they will motivate themselves to achieve their goals. For instance, sign up for a class, exercise with a friend, or buy a new racquet when goal achieved. (15 minutes)

      a. See pages 238 and 239 of the workbook.

      b. Have them share their goals and method of motivating themselves in groups of three or four. Encourage the small groups to give feedback.

      c. Answer questions and invite comments when the large group reconvenes.

    5. Give suggestions for keeping at their exercise program and avoiding injury. (5 minutes)

(See pages 241 and 242 of the workbook and Chapter 19 of this guide.)

(10-minute break)

  C. Deep Relaxation (20 minutes)

Follow the seven suggestions for relaxation described in the One Three-Hour Presentation mentioned earlier in this chapter.

  D. Nutrition (30 minutes)

    1. See Chapter 18 in the workbook and guide.

    2. Give a lecture on Nutrition basics.

    3. Exercise: Have your students write from memory what they typically ingest during the course of a day, including drugs such as alcohol, nicotine, and caffeine.

2. Exercise: Have your students write down at least three ways that they would like to improve their diet and suggest that they set these as goals for the next two weeks. Ask them to also write down how they will motivate themselves to achieve their nutrition goals. Have your students share their nutrition goals and motivators in groups of three or four. Encourage the small groups to give feedback. Invite questions and comments when group reconvenes.

(lunch break)

III. *Take an active role in shaping your environment*
   A. Ten steps to effective time management drawn from Chapter 13 of the workbook and this guide. (60 minutes)

(10-minute break)

   B. Assertiveness Training
   1. Teach the difference between Aggressive, Passive, and Assertive communication. (30 minutes)
      a. Have your students fill in the blank lines on pages 131 and 132 of the workbook.
      b. Define and give examples of Aggressive, Passive and Assertive styles of communication. (See pages 132 and 135 in the workbook and Chapter 12 of this guide.)
      c. Go over the exercise on pages 136 and 137 of the workbook.
      d. Have your students go over their answers to the "fill in the blanks" exercise to determine which of the three communication styles they are most likely to use.
   2. Three easy steps to setting limits and asking for what you want (30 minutes) (See Short Form Assertiveness Technique on pages 147 and 148 in the workbook.)
   3. Three easy steps to more effective listening (20 minutes)
      a. See pages 149 and 150 in the workbook and Chapter 13 of this guide.
      b. Point out that this is the Short Form Assertiveness Technique in reverse: listening for "I think, I feel, and I want" in what the other person is saying.
   4. Workable Compromise (20 minutes)
      a. See pages 151 and 152 of the workbook.
      b. Explain the concept and demonstrate an example, using role play.

    c. Make clear that Workable Compromise works best when each person has expressed how he thinks and feels about the issue at hand, and what he wants.

    d. Have people break into groups of four where two people practice Workable Compromise at a time.

    e. Take questions and invite comments when the large group reconvenes.

(10-minute break)

  5. Avoid Manipulation (30 to 60 minutes)
See pages 153 to 154 of the workbook and Chapter 12 of this guide.

Day 2

IV. *Take charge of your thoughts*
  A. Explain how "Man is not disturbed by events, but by the view he takes of them." (5 minutes)
(See pages 39 and 100 of the workbook.)

  B. Go over at least the first 10 of the 21 Irrational Beliefs. (30 minutes)
(See pages 105 to 109 in the workbook and Chapter 10 of this guide.)

  C. Go over the Rules to Promote Rational Thinking. (3 to 5 minutes)
(See page 110 in the workbook.)

  D. Teach steps A through E for Refuting Irrational Ideas. (30 to 40 minutes)
(See pages 110 to 114 in the workbook and Chapter 10 of this guide.)

(15-minute break)

  E. Teach Progressive Relaxation. (20 minutes)
(See pages 21 to 25 in the workbook and Chapter 3 in this guide.)

  F. Teach Rational Emotive Imagery. (30 minutes)
(See pages 115 to 117 in the workbook and Chapter 10 of this guide.)

(5-to-10 minute break)

  G. Teach Thought Stopping. (20 to 30 minutes)
(See pages 91 to 97 in the workbook and Chapter 9 of this guide.)

(One hour lunch break)

  H. Teach Coping Skills. (1¼ hours)
(See pages 119 to 129 in the workbook and Chapter 11 of this guide.)

(10-minute break)

I.   Teach Self Hypnosis. (1¼ hours)

1. See pages 65 to 79 in the workbook and Chapter 7 of this guide.

2. The following is a time-efficient outline:
   a. Introduction: Emphasize that when a person is in a relaxed state he is more open to positive, healthful suggestions.

   b. Demonstrate suggestibility by taking your class through an exercise on postural sway.

   c. Teach the elements of good hypnotic suggestions. Give several examples of hypnotic suggestions for relaxation and stress management. Have your students write out three suggestions for themselves.

   d. Describe the basic elements of a hypnotic induction as well as deepening techniques.

   e. Take them through a hypnotic induction in which you use the basic elements and deepening techniques that you described. When they are sufficiently in trance, suggest that they repeat to themselves several times and very slowly one of their own hypnotic suggestions.

   f. Give them a written form of this hypnotic induction for them to read into an audio tape recorder, along with their own hypnotic suggestions, to practice at home.

   g. Invite comments and questions on self hypnosis.

V. *Summary (15 minutes)*

   A. Highlight the important points that you presented in your introduction the first day.

   B. Show your students how to use the Symptom Effectiveness Chart on pages 12 and 13 in the workbook.

   C. Stress that practice of these techniques on a regular basis for at least a month will help to establish habits of effective stress management and relaxation.

   D. Invite questions and comments.